Happiness in Recovery

by Margaret Hart

Disclaimer: The contents of this book are for general information purposes only and are in no way intended to constitute personal medical or professional advice. Readers are advised to take professional advice that is specific to their individual situation. Neither the publisher nor author shall be held liable for any loss or damages to the reader resulting from the information contained herein.

ISBN: 978-1-68418-298-5

Published by the Sovereign Media Group.

© 2016 All rights reserved

No part of the publication may be reproduced, distributed, or transmitted in any form or by any means, including photocopying, recording, or other electronic or mechanical methods, without the prior written permission of the publisher, except in the case of brief quotations embodies in the critical reviews and certain other non-commercial uses permittedby copyright law.

- Author's Note 1
- Preface 3
- Introduction 9
- Defining the problem 11
- The anatomy of happiness 13
- Choosing to be happy in an imperfect world 21
- The process of mind 25
- Step 1. Mind your Mind 35
  - Exercise: "Yes but" (AKA weeding your mental garden) 42
  - Dealing with repetitive negative Self Talk 45
  - Exercise: Affirmations 47
- Step 2. Being Present 51
  - Accepting the reality of now 51
  - Exercise: Observing your breath 57
  - In case of emergency – Breathe 58
  - Subtler points of practice 59
- Step 3. Gratitude 61
  - Reframing your reality 61

- *Gratitude Exercises*..67
  - *Gratitude lists*..67
  - *Expressing gratitude*..68
- *Step 4. Forgiveness*..69
  - *Self Forgiveness*..76
  - *Seeking the pardon of others*..........................78
  - *Exercise: Practicing forgiveness*......................80
- *Step 5. Generosity*...83
  - *The Dumpster Diver*..85
  - *The Big Tipper*..85
  - *Exercise: Practicing Generosity*.......................86
- *Step 6. Kindness and Compassion*.......................89
  - *Exercise: Practising compassion*......................90
  - *Kindness*...90
  - *Exercise: Practicing kindness*...........................91
- *Step 7. Active Self Care*..95
  - *Physical Exercise*...97
  - *Improving your diet*..98
  - *Finding community*..99

Pain Management..*100*

A mental exercise for dealing with pain...................*102*

Mental Illness..*106*

Resources..*108*

Cognitive Behavioural Therapy..............................*108*

Addiction and Recovery Programs..........................*110*

Rational and Secular Programs..............................*110*

Spiritual based Recovery Programs.........................*115*

Mindfulness and Meditation Courses......................*116*

Guidelines for practice..*118*

Hope for PTSD sufferers...*119*

Author's Note..*123*

Author's Note

I would like to take just a moment to personally thank you for purchasing this book. Your time is so precious and I feel both honoured and privileged that you have deemed this work worthy of your time and attention.

It is my sincere hope that you may find something within these pages that can help you in both your personal relationships and your day-to-day life.

If you find value in this book it would be greatly appreciated if you could help others find it, so that they too can benefit. Leaving a review on Amazon only takes a few moments but it is extremely helpful in guiding others (who may also benefit from it) towards this book.

Be Happy

Preface

When I sat down to write this book I asked myself "What qualifies me to write a book on happiness?" People's time is precious and if I am going to ask someone to invest their time in reading my book then I had better be able to offer them something of real value.

While many friends have told me that I offer wise and soothing council, I am not a trained therapist nor do I have any clinical expertise in dealing with the miseries of the human mind; so how can I be so bold as to put myself forward to speak on this subject?

The short answer is that I am a genuinely happy person. That's not to say that things always go the way I want them to, or that I don't have my off days. Sure, my life has its share of disappointments and I get a bit ratty now and again, but overall I wake up with a smile and I wish everyone well.

But it wasn't always like that. My happiness has been hard won. Like most people my life has not always been easy. I don't talk about it much these days but my childhood was characterised by violence, verbal and physical abuse, bullying, ridicule, isolation and a deep and overwhelming sense of despair. By the age of 10 I had spent many an hour seriously contemplating suicide. Such was the violence in my home that I was convinced I would die by my father's hand before I was old enough to set out on my own.

After a particularly gruelling incident with a shotgun, (from which I thankfully escaped unharmed), I left home at the age of 15. Under skilled and underprepared for life I launched myself out into the world; but in spite of my having escaped my abuser my existential pain remained acute. My life did not, as I had expected, instantly transform into a sea of bliss; instead years of depression, PTSD and addiction followed.

Even though I was unable to get a job, I did manage to keep my life together on the surface. By the time I was 16 I had started a small second hand business in an empty shop front. While this kept me alive I was still desperate for love and companionship, so I got myself a dog.

Preface

What I am about to share with you now is the most shameful moment of my life; and it is, without question, the worst thing I have ever done.

I had been out working in my shop and had left my new puppy at home. I had put out a tray of dirt and newspaper for the dog to toilet on, but when I got home I discovered the dog had pushed the paper to one side and relieved herself in the middle of the rug. An overpowering fury welled up inside of me. My foot left the ground and travelled through the air to meet the belly of my new friend. Even though the whole thing seemed to happen in slow motion I couldn't stop it. I was kicking the dog!

I was 16 and I had hit rock bottom. Throughout my childhood I had told my self I was nothing like my father, that I could never be so beastly; and yet there I was, foot flying through the air, taking my frustrations out on an innocent, powerless being who was in my care!

No sooner had my foot reached the dog, than my legs gave way and I collapsed to the floor in flood of tears. In that moment it became crystal clear to me, I carried the exact same potential as my father. That the afflictions that had brought him so low were as much mine as they were his, and for all my righteous denial I was equally capable of such terrible acts. The only real difference between my father and myself was 40 years and a lot of alcohol.

As I lay sprawled out on the floor I looked into the forgiving eyes of my little puppy friend and made a solemn promise. No matter how hard it would be and no matter how long it took, I would not allow this toxic legacy to rule my world. I would find a way to purge myself of the capricious impulses that had so possessed and tortured my father.

From that moment forward my life would be a quest to do better.

Over the years I have travelled many roads and encountered many dead ends in the hope of finding answers. I have faced down many a wild storm that has raged through my mind and I have endured moments when the pain of my life was so overwhelming I thought I would surely go insane.

I have self-abused, self-medicated, raked over my tales of woe in a therapist's office, travelled all of the

12 steps and done countless affirmations. I have pawed over the Bible, the Koran, the Analects, the Bhagavad Gita, the Tripitaka, the Mahayana Sutras, and the Lao Tzu. I have sort to heal my body and sooth my mind with everything from NLP, CBT, the Landmark forum, Hakomi therapy, shiatsu, rolfing, re-birthing, acupuncture, yoga, hypnotherapy, transactional analysis, encounter groups and many different types of meditation.

Throughout my journey I have been sorely tested by some and graciously helped by many others, but I have persisted on my course. I have learnt that deep change takes time and one needs to be both patient and persistent; for no matter where one is on the path, one simply needs to keep moving forward and eventually one's progress will become apparent.

Over time I have come to see that the answers I sought are all disarmingly simple, practical, non-sectarian and universally applicable; and that anyone who works persistently to improve the tone and quality of their mind has the capacity to be much happier, regardless of religion, gender, age, race, or life circumstance.

As someone who has taken a few steps on the path of happiness, my aim with this book is to provide a practical, clear and helpful guide to moving forward on that path and to offer some genuine hope and help to all those who continue to suffer as acutely as I once did.

It is my sincere wish that anyone who takes the time to read this book will come away armed with the tools to ease their pains and build a happier world, both for the good of themselves and the good of others.

I humbly request that you work diligently on your self-improvement and take care to be gentle and kind with yourself and others in the process. I wish you well on your journey.

Sincerely Margaret

Introduction

None of us are totally alone in our miseries. The simple fact is everyone suffers. No matter how much we might wish it no-one can avoid some measure of disappointment, suffering and misfortune in their life, and no-one can feel on top of the world 100% of the time.

That said, some people are clearly much happier than others.

So what do these "happy" people have in common? what is their secret? Happy people dwell in both palaces and slums, they are of all races; they are men and women, young and old, healthy and infirm, and some are beautiful while others are quite homely.

If you look at the surface of their lives there seems to be no common factor at all. However these "happy" people were not just tapped on the head at birth by mystical happy fairies. If we look deeper, into their hearts and minds, the secret starts to reveal it's self, and it's no accident!

Happy people make good mental choices, and they practice good mental habits.

The good news is you can learn to do what they do; and as you practice, over time you will become just like them. A much happier person!

In the following chapters I will not only examine the problems in our thinking and reactions that lead to our unhappiness, I will outline a number of clear practical steps you can take to significantly improve your level of happiness.

There will no doubt be obstacles, such as old mental habits and conditioning that will dog your progress, but if you muster your determination and keep moving forward you are bound to be successful.

Be happy

Defining the problem

Sure, we all have our off days, days where we just don't feel the joy of being alive, but for some those grey days can vastly outnumber the good days. For some people the malaise can become so prominent that life becomes a hard joyless grind of pushing one's self forward, day after day, with little reward or relief.

It is at this point that many of us start actively looking for ways to ease our pain. Trouble is that often times many of the things we turn to make our situation considerably worse.

We either abandon the reigns of self-control and launch ourselves into a life of self-harm, (indulging in things like drugs and alcohol, anger, violence, lying, stealing, gambling, comfort eating, sexual misconduct, criminality etc.), or we try to purge our existential angst by subjecting ourselves (and others) to crippling, unobtainable levels of austerity and self control.

But ultimately neither the party animal nor the monk has fixed his problem. While at the surface level we may feel some mild short-term relief, we cannot escape the nagging sense that all is not quite as it should be in the deeper levels of our mind, and many times we find ourselves suffering a smorgasbord of negative consequences on top of our original problem.

What is needed is a deep and lasting solution, a practical set of tools and methods to ease our suffering; a set of simple steps that can be practiced by anyone regardless of age, race, religion or life circumstances. This is the blueprint this book aims to provide.

The anatomy of happiness

If you ask people **"do you want to be happy?"** Almost without exception you will get a resounding **"YES"**.

But what does it actually mean to be happy? This question has been asked throughout the ages, but in spite of the fact that happiness tops most people's list of desires very few people seem to have a solid notion of what it actually is.

One commonly held belief is that happiness involves an uninterrupted flow of pleasurable feelings and experiences.

But does the idea of endless pleasure have any reality?

Pleasure by its very nature can only ever be fleeting. On a biochemical level we only feel pleasure when we do something that triggers our brain's reward system and we experience a surge in the neurotransmitter dopamine. When we get that rush of euphoria we naturally want to go out and do whatever it was we just did over and over again, but unfortunately for us our brains are adaptive. When we repeat a pleasurable behaviour too often our brain responds by shutting down our dopamine receptors so we get progressively less and less of a reward. This is the biological underpinning of tolerance and addiction, which as we all know is not a path to happiness. The unfortunate truth is that endless pleasure is not something our human biology can sustain.

So if endless pleasure is not the seat of happiness, then what is?

Ask a thousand people to define what they think would make them happy and you will get a thousand different answers. For some it would be finding a partner, a new pair of shoes, having their health or loosing 50lbs, for others it could be having their house paid off or maybe just having a house to live in.

Whatever the individual details, for most of us the answer lies in getting something we don't currently have. (This is hardly surprising considering the countless millions advertisers spend bombarding us with the notion that there is something missing).

The idea that happiness can be achieved by obtaining "the missing thing" is a powerfully seductive notion. It provides us with a reason for our current lack of happiness -the absence of the desired thing- it gives us the (false) promise of a cure and it provides a concrete point of focus for all our efforts. And let's face it, without something to aim for life could feel pretty hopeless.

But is the "missing thing" really the problem?

How many times have you wanted something, I mean REALLY wanted it, burned for it, believed you could never be happy without out it? Only to find that once you had the coveted object the joy was short lived and it failed make any lasting impact on your happiness.

Children are regularly afflicted by this kind of rampant desire, they want the latest Xbox, smart phone, sneakers etc… and seriously, they will DIE if they don't get it. But almost immediately upon obtaining the object of their desire it loses all taste and they move on the next "must have" item.

And this endless craving is not limited to money or objects, it can be directed towards people, power or prestige *"If only I could go out with X", "if only so and so would like me", or "if only I could have that job or win that award"*, if only, if only if only… it just goes on and on.

If you run your mind back over your life and think of all the things you wanted and then got one thing becomes very clear: **True and lasting happiness can not be achieved simply by getting what we want.**

So, if we cannot experience an endless flow of pleasant feelings and getting what we want doesn't make us happy, is a true and lasting happiness even possible?

The answer depends largely on how you define happiness. If your concept of happiness is wedded to acquisitiveness or *"feeling based"* definitions like ecstatic, elated, jubilant and exhilarated then the answer is probably not. Sure, you can have moments of that kind of happiness, but they will be fleeting, for no matter how hard we might try we can never hang onto a good feeling. It will last as long as it lasts, but we have absolutely no control over how long that is.

However if you choose to favour the more useful, attainable *"attitude based"* definitions such as content, satisfied, cheerful, upbeat, sunny and gratified then it is technically possible to be happy no matter what life dishes up.

The fact is human existence is beset with problems. No matter who you are or how good you have it there are always obstacles to overcome. Everyone gets sick from time to time, everyone suffers setbacks and everyone eventually loses loved ones. Unwanted things happen, wanted things do not happen. Even if we get something we want the nature of the world is such that we will eventually lose it.

But this doesn't mean we can never be happy. What it does mean however is that if we are to be happy we will have to accept that our life will never be a perfect unchanging experience. Any enduring sense of happiness will need to accommodate both the highs and the lows and carry us through the good days and the bad.

True happiness does not depend on what we have or what happens to us. True happiness is an attitude. It is a choice we make about how we see the world and what we bring to it.

Misery loves a reason

People give many reasons for not being happy but mostly we attribute our misery to something that has occurred outside of ourselves. Anything that happens out in the big wide world that we do not like and we immediately jump into the victim suit, *"if he hadn't abused me; if I hadn't lost my job; if my nose were smaller; if, if, if… then I wouldn't be so unhappy"*. On the face of it these arguments appear to have some merit but is it really true?

Unwanted things happen to everyone. Do you know of anyone who leads a life totally devoid of disappointment or conflict? It's just not possible to control the world so that we always get what we want or so that nobody ever insults, abuses, refuses or denies us.

However it is possible to change our set of responses; and if we respond differently, we feel differently.

By way of an example, I had recently arranged to meet a friend for lunch. As she walked out of her front door that morning she realized her car wasn't where she had left it. After the moment of shock, it sank in. Her car had been stolen. She turned up to our lunch date about 30 minutes late on her bicycle, smiling broadly.

Why was she smiling in spite of her obvious misfortune? It's quite simple. While most of us would have been totally focused on the great loss we had suffered, she opened the conversation with *"I'm so glad I've got a bicycle"*.

Instead of cursing the thieves over and over in her mind, she had chosen to focus on the fact she had alternate mode of transport, and **how lucky she was!** I'm not saying she wasn't at all disappointed or annoyed, but to her way of thinking the car was gone & there was nothing she could do about it, so she made a conscious choice not to dwell on the negative.

Was she unlucky to have had her car stolen, or lucky to have secondary mode of transport? The truth is, if she believes she is unlucky she is, and if she believes she is lucky she is! The choice is hers and hers alone.

Fortunately eliminating all unpleasantness and conflict from our lives is not a necessary ingredient of happiness *(and also manifestly impossible)*, however managing our thinking is. Rarely do we attribute our unhappiness to the way we are thinking about things, but for the most part our way of thinking or framing our world is the root cause of our misery.

Choosing to be happy in an imperfect world

One of the most common reasons people give for their unhappiness is that the world is so truly awful, so full of suffering and pain, that one would have to be a blind fool to be happy in a world such as this.

This may seem a pretty convincing argument and to a certain degree it is true, the world is imperfect and people often do awful things to each other. You never have to look very far to find someone being dishonest, selfish, angry, greedy or cruel.

Some people feel that to be happy in the face of such human failings would be living in denial or mean that they lacked compassion or empathy, or are somehow ignorant of the plight of those who suffer at the hands others. But if one looks closely at what is the root cause of people's bad behaviour it becomes so clear. People only behave badly when they are not happy.

No one steals unless they want something they do not have. No one lies unless they are unhappy with the truth. Happy people do not erupt into violence. Happy people do not kill, rape, abuse or disregard others.

All human folly arises as a result of people not being happy, either because they want something they do not have, they don't want something they do have, or they want to feel a way they do not feel.

It is no small irony that many people feel they cannot be happy when there are so many people in the world behaving with such appallingly disregard for others. But when you get right down to it, it is a profound lack of happiness that is the root cause of all antisocial behaviour.

If you search your memory for the all times when you have acted in a less than noble fashion you will pretty soon realise it's true. All of your lowest acts were born out of a deep sense of desire or dissatisfaction. No one ever harms others unless they are covetous, unsettled or miserable within themselves.

Conversely happy people are loving, kind, generous, helpful and compassionate; all the things the world needs more of. Happy people consider others. Happy people go out of their way to help others. Happy people feel full and content and have plenty left over for others. All the best things people do are the product of happiness, good will and a generosity of spirit.

There is a famous social worker in my city who runs outreach programs for the homeless. Every year he holds a noted fund raising raffle. Last year, much to the amusement of the press, he announced the prizes. Third prize was a weekend away, second prize was a new luxury car, and the first prize was a week working unpaid at the homeless shelter kitchen. When the press quizzed him about how he could offer a first prize that *"wasn't worth anything"*, he smiled deeply and gave this reply *"I can tell you with absolute certainty that the 1st prize winner will get one thousand times more happiness than the 2nd or 3rd prize winners; and the joy of their experience will stay with them for a lifetime. The winner of the new car will only be happy for about a week"*

More handwringing dissatisfaction and unhappiness can never be a cure for the existential and behavioural problems of humanity. True happiness is the only real cure for humanity's bad behaviour. It is only though being truly happy that we can be our best selves and give our best service to others.

If we human beings are to continue to evolve and thrive as a species we seriously need to get happy.

It is our duty, not just to ourselves but also to the rest of the world, to be as happy as we can.

The process of mind

For most people the workings of the human mind are a complete mystery. How our thoughts and feelings arise is not something we are accustomed to questioning. Instead we tend to set ourselves on autopilot, accepting whatever arises in our mind without any further thought or inquiry.

But if our thoughts and feelings don't always serve our best interests is it wise to unquestioningly accept whatever pops into our heads? How do we know what is real and what is imagined? How do we know our minds are not deceiving us?

Occasionally we all fall prey to toxic thinking and without the ability to rationally detach we can be pretty severely knocked around by our negative thoughts.

But how can we detach ourselves from our negative thinking? To find an answer we need to rationally examine the process by which our mind experiences and responds to the world.

While our minds are undoubtedly subtle and complex, at a very rudimentary level we can break down our cognitive and sensory functioning into four basic processes.

Cognition:

To Cognise: verb cognised, cognising.

> 1. to perceive; become conscious of; know.

As human beings we are equipped with several senses that allow us to receive sensory inputs, such as sight, sound, touch, taste, smell, and *-although it is rarely understood to be a sensory input-* thought. *(I will explain shortly why thought needs to be considered a sensory input).*

Whenever any form of sensory stimulation arrives at one of our sense doors the mind is instantly "cognisant" of the occurrence. We are aware that "something" has occurred.

Recognition:

To recognise: verb, recognised, recognising.

1.to identify as something previously seen, known, etc.:

2.to identify from knowledge of appearance or characteristics:

As soon as our mind is alerted to an occurrence, it dives into our memory to assess the incoming information against what we have on record.

By the time we are three to five years old we have some kind of reference for practically everything we encounter. Even if we do not explicitly "recognise" an input, we are able to recognise enough about it to put into a broad category.

For example when looking at a woman we may not know her personally but we recognise that she is human, female, blonde, short, thin, a police officer etc. We may not recognise a song but we know that it is music, that it is loud, guitar based, male voiced and heavy metal.

As soon as the mind is satisfied it has recognised the input and has some kind of reference point it moves on to the next stage.

Evaluation:

To evaluate: verb, evaluated, evaluating.

1. to determine or set the value or amount of; appraise:

2. to judge or determine the significance, worth, or quality of; to assess:

There are many degrees and gradations, but the mind will sort all inputs into one of two basic categories, good or bad. I like it or I don't like it.

Once the mind has assigned a value to an input according to desirability it immediately moves on to the next process.

Reaction:

Reaction: noun

1. action in response to some influence, event, etc.:

2. Physiology. action in response to a stimulus, as of the system or of a nerve, muscle, etc.

The Process of Mind

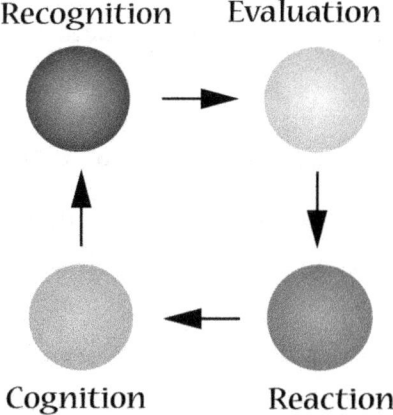

While there are a vast number of possible reactions we may have in response to a given event, our reactions can be broadly described in one of two ways. We react with either craving or aversion.

If our mind's evaluation is positive we want more, if the mind's evaluation is negative we want less. We want more sugar, less pain, more compliments, less insults; no matter what has occurred all of our reactions can be distilled down into a base of either craving or aversion.

Logically it follows that when our mind is in the process of reacting it is always in a state of dissatisfaction. It is simply not possible to "react" in a neutral objective way. If our mind remains neutral and objective with whatever stimuli it receives then there is no reaction, just observation and awareness.

It is in the process of reaction that all our troubles start. Be it lust, greed, hatred, addiction, anxiety etc., all afflictive emotions arise as reactions in the mind.

But it doesn't stop there. Whatever our reaction may be it instantly gives rise to more sensations throughout the body and the process immediately repeats itself, our sensations feeding our reactions and our reactions in turn feeding our sensations.

But what exactly are we reacting to?

On the surface it appears we are reacting to the sensory objects outside of ourselves, but is that really the case? If our reactions are really determined by the quality and nature of a sensory object then it would be perfectly logical to assume that all people would have the same reaction to all things. But people can have manifestly different reactions to the same object. While some people like oysters others hate them, so clearly it is not the inherent quality of the oyster that determines its desirability but rather our personal reaction to it.

So what exactly are we reacting to? If the oyster itself is not determining our reaction then what is?

If we review the four basic processes of mind it is clear that the quality and tone of our reactions is the product of our mind's evaluation process. If our evaluation says the oyster is good, we respond with craving and desire, if it says it is bad we respond with hatred and aversion.

But we need to take it one step further and ask what information does the mind's evaluation process use to make the call? Why does your mind decide oysters are good while my mind decides they are bad? What is actually informing that evaluation? We know it is not the oyster because if it were everyone would make the same evaluation. So if not the oyster itself, then what?

To answer that we need to take another step back in the process and look at what happens whenever anything comes in contact with one of our senses.

How does our mind know something has actually occurred?

The simple answer is because whenever anything arrives at one of our sense doors a sensation arises within the body. My hand touches the table and a sensation arises. The perfume of a flower enters my nose and a sensation arises. An attractive person enters my field of vision and a sensation arises. A tune comes on the radio and a sensation arises. An oyster lands on my tongue and a sensation arises and our minds are constantly attuned to all these sensations.

When you look into it deeply it becomes so clear, it is the sensations that arise inside our bodies that our minds are actually evaluating and reacting to, not the external objects.

This is why our thoughts must also be considered sensory inputs, because the moment a thought enters the mind a sensation arises in the body, and we in turn react to that sensation.

Have you ever found yourself embarrassed, despondent, anxious or tense because of something you have thought? Has a thought ever brought a tear to your eye?

If we think about a great loss or set back that we have suffered it will automatically give rise to difficult, unpleasant sensations in the body.

Whenever we are beset with afflictive emotions there is always a physical sensation that we are reacting to. We are hot under the collar, sick to our stomachs, trembling with fear. In fact many milder mental disorders, such as low-level depression and anxiety are caused by our reactions to the rush of hormones and chemicals that flood our system when we indulge in toxic thinking.

This is the how the mind-body interaction works:

The objects of our sense doors *(including our thoughts)* **give rise to our feelings** *(sensations)***, and our feelings/sensations give rise to our reactions.**

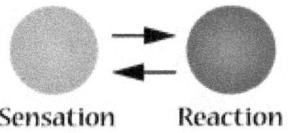

Sensation   Reaction

When we are reacting our actions are beyond our control. How many times have you heard someone say, "I just lost it" or "I reacted very badly" when they have lost control and done something questionable?

Of the four basic processes of mind cognition, recognition and evaluation are benign. It is our reactions that cause us all of our miseries, and for most of us reaction is by far the dominant habit pattern of the mind.

The good news is that it is possible to learn to practice mindful non-reaction, and as one continues to practice one automatically becomes happier and happier, and less and less reactive.

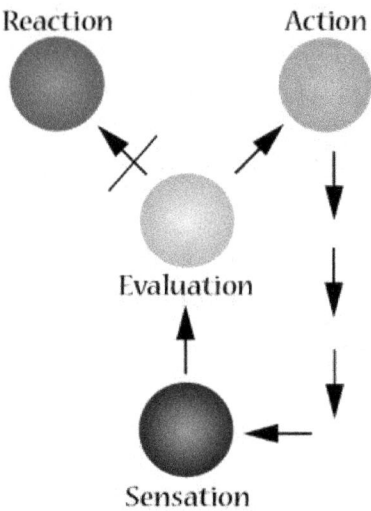

When we stop reacting, we become free to act. Unlike our reactions, over which we have no choice or power, our actions are always the product of our conscious choice. And when we choose consciously, from a point of happiness, we will always choose a noble path, which is good for ourselves and good for others.

When we learn how to unshackle ourselves from our reactions and be happy with whatever sensations arise we become truly free.

Step 1.

Mind your Mind

Many people believe that our feelings occur automatically in response to things around us and that we are merely the passive recipients of whatever feelings arise. On the surface of things this may appear to be true but is it really the case?

Certainly when someone abuses us it feels very unpleasant; a well of anger rises in us and it feels like we have no control over it at all. But if our being abused is truly the cause of our unhappiness then surely once the abuse has stopped our bad feelings would go too?

But this is rarely the case. Instead we use the abuse to nurture bad thoughts and feelings within our own minds. Think about it. How long did the abuse last? Maybe 30 seconds? And how long does your ill feeling last? 5 minutes, a day, a week, a month or maybe even more?

We repeat the incident over and over on the stage of our mind. *"he said this, she said that"*, and with each rerun our torment is inflamed yet again. It is not until we actually stop running the replay that our bad feelings begin to subside. And to make matters worse we are not running this replay as an objective observer. We overlay it with our own meaning and commentary. And quite often we are dead wrong!

An unpleasant thought may or may not be accurate but the autopilot of the mind does not stop for a fact check, it just assumes the offending thought is 100% true and reacts accordingly.

For example a thought like *"Nobody likes me"*, could cause a cascade of hideous sensations to oscillate throughout one's body, leaving one drenched in unhappiness. If one had such a thought and took it as true without question it could easily make one defensive, prickly, combative or even rude; behaviours that could easily make people respond as if they do not like you.

I remember one time I was at a conference. At the start of the lunch break I was approached by a woman I knew vaguely. She stepped in front of me and began to chat. I smiled politely and excused myself, informing her I had to get the bathroom. Suddenly her face turned sour, she hissed, *"You're a liar just like all the rest, if you don't want to talk to me at least have the decency to be honest about it"*.

I was totally stunned, *"No"*, I assured her "I will come back, I just really need to use the bathroom". Rolling her eyes she let out a giant sigh *"don't bother"*, then turned on her heel and stomped off. *"Wow, that woman is really suffering"* I thought as I raced to the bathroom. As I sat in the cubicle I felt a great deal of compassion for her. It must be awful to truly believe no one wants to talk to you. I also contemplated the fact that as a result of her outburst I actually didn't want to go back and talk to her for my own pleasure *(but I did have an overwhelming wish to see her feeling better)*.

Later, another woman who had witnessed the incident came up to me. She told me in intricate detail how the same woman had been unbelievably rude to her on a previous occasion and that she knew how upset I must be because she herself had been upset **for days** afterward.

Both of these women were upset because they believed things that simply weren't true and then responded to them as if they were true beyond all doubt. The first woman believed no one wanted to talk to her and that I had shunned and rejected her. The second woman believed the only response one could have to such an incident was to be "really upset".

Just because you think it doesn't make it true!

For centuries people thought the world was flat and indeed it seemed to be so. People believed that man would never fly, let alone walk on the moon. Thousands of people have been wrongly convicted because juries thought they were guilty. People think all kinds of things that simply are not true.

If we take a scientific approach and examine our beliefs objectively, really look at the evidence for both for and against what we believe, we will most likely find that we hold several beliefs that cannot conclusively be proven to be true. And yet, even though we are unable to verify the truth of our beliefs, we respond as if these "beliefs" are true beyond all doubt.

Tuning your filter.

Have you ever played punch buggy? It's a game my niece taught me where every time you see a VW Beetle the first person to say "punch buggy" gets to playfully *(and gently)* punch their opponent in the arm. My first response to my niece's suggestion that we play this game was *"but there are almost no Beetles left on the road"*. Boy was I wrong, there are thousands of them out there! But until I started looking I just never noticed them.

Every second we are bombarded with sensory information and it is totally crucial to our survival that we prioritise that information and filter much of it out. If we didn't the world would become totally overwhelming. However what we often fail to realise is that we are actively filtering the world according to our beliefs and preferences. For example my husband sees motorbikes everywhere he goes, whereas I see unique and distinctive architecture.

But it's not only material things that we filter; we also filter our thoughts. Whether we realise it or not we are not passive players in the drama of our minds, we actively choose which thoughts we believe and which thoughts we reject, and we then respond accordingly.

The tale of the two travellers and the old woman:

A traveller came upon an old woman resting by the roadside. *"What sort of people live in the next town?"* asked the traveller.

"What were the people like where you've come from?" queried the old woman.

"They were terrible; the most disagreeable, argumentative, lazy, selfish people in the world. I couldn't wait to leave"

"Really?" the old woman questioned.

"Oh yes, they were a really bad lot".

The old woman let out a sympathetic sigh. *"Well, I'm afraid that you'll find the much same sort of people in the next town".*

Disappointed, the traveller continued on her way.

Some time later another traveller, coming from the same direction stopped to talk to the old woman.

"What sort of people live in the next town?" she asked.

"What were the people like in the town you've come from?" the old woman queried once again.

"They were the best people in the world. Hard working, honest, and friendly. I'm sorry to be leaving them." Answered the second traveller.

"Fear not," said the old woman. *"You'll find the same sort of people in the next town."*

The old woman in this parable was wise indeed. She understood that what each traveller believed would determine what she would find.

What comes first, the evidence or the belief?

As an example: the woman at the conference, who thought that no one wanted to talk to her, responded as if that thought were an unassailable truth. She could not see that her belief *(that no one wanted to talk to her)* had led to her being unpleasant, which in turn seeded the response that she was expecting. And of course as it turned out she was right, after being given a mouthful I really didn't want to talk to her.

We may not be able to stop negative thoughts arising but we certainly have the ability to determine which of our thoughts to believe and which to reject.

The choices we make will effect how we feel and respond and our responses will in turn determine what the world throws back at us.

If you truly believe that you are ugly and someone tells you that you are beautiful, you are far more likely to believe that they are patronizing or lying than that you are wrong. If you believe they are lying then you are likely to distrust or suspect them or maybe even confront them; a stance that will undoubtedly colour any future relations between you.

Exercise: "Yes but" *(AKA weeding your mental garden).*

This is a very simple exercise. Every time you find yourself afflicted by a negative thought, weed it out and plant a positive thought to counter it.

There is a wise old woman I know who has built her life around this exercise. She is 91, legally blind, half deaf and practically crippled with arthritis. But if you mentioned any of this to her she would reply with, *"Yes but, I am warm and well fed, and get to see my family everyday and spend my time doing things I love and I haven't got cancer!"*

If you tried to commiserate with her over the fact she can no longer read she would say, *"Yes but there are such a lot of interesting programs on the radio".*

It doesn't matter what happens she will always find a positive. When she got kidney stones and was doubled over in agony for a couple of weeks, all she had to say about it was, *"I am so lucky I don't have to wait months for the operation"*

Unlike so many elderly people here in the West this wise old woman doesn't live in a nursing home, she lives with her family. Even her son-in-law adores her and spends countless happy hours chatting with her.

Her phone rings non-stop, to which she quips with a wry smile, *"I cannot do a lot for people these days, but I have two good ears and I can listen, and people need to be heard".*

This old lady can hardly walk, is practically blind and is in constant pain, but is she beset with misery? No. She is the most relentlessly glass-half-full person I have ever known. But she will tell you herself that it's no accident, she has to consciously work at it. Whenever she catches herself starting to feel sorry for herself or dwelling on her misfortunes she pulls herself up sharply and finds a positive counter thought to fix her mind to.

There is no lonely old age for this woman. Her determination to dwell on the positive and reflect her joy and enthusiasm back into the world means that she is constantly surrounded by friends and loved ones.

Choosing to invest your mental energy in a positive outlook doesn't mean that you are ignorant of the facts, or that you are unaware of the imperfect nature of things. It simply means that you are making an active choice about how you frame your world.

Like the woman who had her car stolen and her choice to rest her mind on the fact she had another means of transport, we can all direct our mind towards happier thoughts. If you practice taking the **"yes but"** approach to your misfortunes you will find yourself smiling a lot more and crying a lot less.

Dealing with repetitive negative Self Talk: Calming the beast within.

We all talk to ourselves constantly. We are both the narrator and the listener in the mind's internal conversation; a conversation that runs nonstop throughout our waking hours.

Depending on the tone and tenor of this conversation it can be either your best friend or your worst enemy.

Unfortunately many of us suffer from a relentless stream of negative self-talk that can seriously harm our chances of happiness. These damaging thoughts run endless loops in our minds and are repeated so often that they can start to seem true beyond question.

"I am ugly, I am fat, I am stupid, no one loves me, I am a no talent, I am a fraud, I will never get anywhere, everyone hates me... etc."

If our parents lacked the ability to nurture us properly we may have been fed on a steady diet of negativity from early childhood. It is not unusual for us to take on the negative things we were told about ourselves as children and continually repeat them back to ourselves throughout our lives. For many of us this kind of negative self-talk is so ingrained that it feels totally normal and we continue to berate ourselves internally without ever challenging those thoughts.

But once we truly understand that our thoughts are a major cause of our unhappiness the benefits of adjusting our thinking becomes quite clear.

Human beings are creatures of habit. If we do not actively intervene in our thoughts or behaviours we will continue to think and do what we have always done.

When we go to the gym we understand that it is through the process of repetition that we become stronger. We fully accept that when we practice an exercise over and over again our muscles will become used to the movement; and what may have seemed difficult and uncomfortable at the start will eventually become easy and natural.

We fail to realise that the same principal applies to our habitual self-talk. If we practice repeating any thought over and over, giving it energy and strength, we will reach the point where it becomes habitual and seems true beyond all doubt.

Exercise: Affirmations

If we can recognise that our negative self-talk is the result of repetition, it is only logical to assume that new habitual modes of self-talk can be achieved by the same method.

This is a simple exercise, but it does take perseverance.

Monitor your thoughts. Make a note of any distressing thoughts that seem particularly prevalent, such as *"no body likes me"* for example, then consciously bring up a thought that directly counters it, such as *"I like myself, and others like me too"*. Whenever the thought *"nobody likes me"* enters your mind consciously reject it and bring up the counter thought.

At first this may seem silly or feel just plain wrong. We may believe with all our heart that no one likes us and that our counter thought is a stupid lie.

The thing we often fail to realise is that if we are carrying such damaging thoughts about ourselves we may well be behaving in ways that people don't like. But it is worth bearing in mind that we are not our behaviour. If our thoughts change our behaviours will automatically change too; and when our behaviours change people will automatically respond to us differently.

If we actively guide our thinking towards better thought patterns eventually, with continued practice, it will become a habit and it will come to feel perfectly natural and right.

If you find your mind is constantly flooded with negative thoughts you may find it beneficial to take this exercise one step further by consciously repeating the counter thoughts over and over to yourself.

If you are seriously afflicted, and find it difficult to challenge or dismiss your negative thoughts you may even choose to write lines to anchor a new positive thinking in place. When I first began my healing journey I wrote at about 20 pages of lines a day for about six months. It felt very odd at first, but over time I found I was much less plagued by my habitual negative thoughts.

This exercise requires diligence. The mind's habit patterns are deeply held; reprogramming years of negative self-talk will not happen overnight, but if you are persistent you will succeed.

To download a FREE list of common affirmations you can use to combat negative self talk just visit the website:

www.thinkhappy.info/freegift.html

Step 2.

Being Present

Accepting the reality of now

Any rational person knows that it is impossible to arrange the world so it is always to her liking. We cannot avoid getting sick. We cannot avoid life's disappointments. This is the reality of our human existence and resistance to that fact is utterly futile.

Fortunately for us there is another reality:

The reality of change!

Nothing is permanent in this world. There is no solid core for us to hang on to. We are all in a constant state of flux, every molecule of our being is changing every moment. Every thought we have or emotion we feel is ephemeral; even if we manage to experience a perfect moment it will inevitably slip away faster than the blink of an eye. And in the end we will all eventually grow old and die. This is the reality for us all.

Feelings and moods ebb and flow like waves on the shore but our mind plays tricks on us. When we are beset by unpleasant feelings we forget that they are impermanent. We get so overwhelmed by our negative emotions we become convinced that unless we **"do something"** we will suffer these miserable feelings forever.

So we either withdraw totally, collapsing into a sea of distraction, self-loathing, self-recrimination and self-medication or we thrash about throwing our misery onto others by lying, stealing, fighting, abusing, betraying, backbiting, blaming and accusing. In our misguided efforts to free ourselves from difficult feelings *(that are, by their very nature, impermanent anyway)* we cause massive damage to others and to ourselves.

Ironically, our inability to ride out our temporary discomfort only ends up stoking the fires of our misery. Be it through addiction, fractured relationships, self-abuse or criminality, waging a war on our more challenging feelings is a lose-lose game.

Have you ever asked yourself in a joyous moment *"how long will this wonderful feeling last"*? Of course not, no one ever questions how long their good feelings will last, we just enjoy them. If we were to raise the question the moment of joy would already be lost.

When negative feelings arise we seem to forget that everything is impermanent and that any pain or misfortune we may suffer is not eternal. We forget that any painful feelings that arise will also pass away.

We do not need to do anything but wait it out.

That is not to say waiting out bad feelings is always easy. It is not. But just like scratching a mosquito bite, fighting your feelings or trying to push them aside with drugs or alcohol will only make the situation much worse.

Imagine your mind is a village and your thoughts and feelings are a river running through it. All kinds of thoughts and feelings flow though your village as you sit on the riverbank watching them pass by.

One day you notice there are some ugly old rotting leaves in your river that you don't like. You decide that you only want to let the sweet clear waters that you love so much flow through your town, so you build a dam and filtration plant upstream.

At first everything seems to be going well. It takes quite a lot of energy and resources to build, but the dam seems to be holding, leaving you free to enjoy that sweet clear flow.

One day you notice that a few of those ugly rotting leaves are polluting your flow again. Upon inspection you realise your dam is now full to the brim with rotting leaves and is starting to over flow, so you decide to build the wall up a bit higher.

There is a nagging thought in the back of your mind telling you that you cannot keep raising the dam wall forever, but you ignore your concerns and set about raising the dam wall anyway. Much to your horror as soon as you have finished raising the dam wall it starts to overflow again; and worse still hairline cracks are starting to appear.

You try desperately to sure up your dam, but no matter what you do the dam continues to bulge and crack under the pressure.

Suddenly there is an almighty crash as your dam gives way. You run screaming from the surging torrent as everything is flattened by a tsunami of rotting leaves. Your lovely village, your beautiful riverbank is totally wiped out; and all that is left a horrible swampy marshland.

This is the reality of fighting your feelings. It is not a fight you can win. No one has the energy or resources to stem the ever-changing tide of thoughts and emotions and any attempt to do so could easily see one addicted, depressed, incarcerated, dysfunctional, lonely, abused *(or abusive)*, only to hit rock bottom with a total mental breakdown.

But what would happen if rather than trying to avoid our difficult feelings we embraced them, invited them in the same way we do with our pleasant feelings, safe in the knowledge that they will pass?

What if, for example, you had remained on the bank observing the river rather than jumping in to try and control the flow? All those unwanted thoughts and feelings would have been carried through your village naturally by the endless current, without any effort or stress on your part.

When you fight something you galvanise and strengthen the thing that you oppose. When you stop fighting and allow life its natural flow you will find yourself lighter, happier and far more equipped to deal with whatever comes your way.

We are so used to reacting to our uncomfortable thoughts and feelings that it is not easy to just "sit on the bank" watching them flow past. But if you can make a habit of such a practice it will profoundly change the way you experience your life.

While it may seem counterproductive to allow our unpleasant feelings to arise and pass away naturally, by doing just that we are actually freeing ourselves from the stress of fighting and the habit of blind reaction. When we observe our thoughts and feelings without reaction we become free to choose our course of action.

But how does one observe without reacting?

Although one may understand the benefits of non-reactive observation at the intellectual level, the natural habit pattern of the mind is always to react. If one is to learn how to observe without reaction then one must have a practical method and practice it until it becomes second nature.

The following exercise is a simple meditation that will help you step back from the fight, be in the moment and embrace the natural flow of thoughts and feelings.

Exercise: Observing your breath.

Sit in a comfortable position, close your eyes and focus all your attention exclusively on the triangular area at the base of the upper lip covering the entire area of nostrils. Try to remain aware of the breath as it passes in and out over this area. Do not try and regulate your breath, just try to keep your attention fixed and observe.

Focusing the mind on the breath helps us in two ways. Firstly it brings our attention wholly into the present moment and secondly by holding our attention firmly on a fixed point of focus we strengthen our ability to choose the course and direction of our mind.

The breath is a wonderful tool for us. It is easy to remain impartial where the breath is concerned; we neither love our breath nor hate it, we simply accept it. Thus observing ones breath without agitation, desire or aversion is a relatively simple and calming practice that strengthens the mind.

When you begin the practice you will notice that your mind is inclined to wander. A thought will come and you will automatically follow it. This is normal and natural so do not feel discouraged or defeated. As soon as you notice your mind has wandered just gently bring it back to your breath.

At first it will be quite difficult as the mind will wander constantly, but with practice you will find your mind becoming more and more stable and you will be able to hold your focus for longer and longer periods. Slowly you will start to develop some measure of mastery over your mind.

In case of emergency:
Breathe ...

The above exercise is especially useful for the times in one's life when things get overwhelming. Sometimes thoughts and emotions well up and we are simply overpowered by them. When you find yourself in danger of being overwhelmed, or harming yourself or others, try to sit quietly and monitor your breath. Remind yourself that constant change is the reality of the universe and what ever has arisen will eventually pass.

No matter how violent and disruptive it may be no storm is eternal. Bad feelings well up, stay for some time, but ultimately they pass away. It may seem counter-intuitive but if you observe them rather than fighting them they will pass by much faster and won't cause you damage on the way through.

You should practice this exercise for at least ten minutes morning and evening *(although the longer you can practice for the more beneficial it will be.)* You can even do this exercise before you get up in the morning or after you have gone to bed at night.

Subtler points of practice

After you have been practicing for some time and find you are able to maintain your focus for at least about one minute –although it could take quite some time to get to that stage- try to develop an awareness of any sensations that crop up on the triangular area starting at the base of the upper lip covering the entire area of nostrils.

Just remain aware of the sensations without reacting to them. You do not need to identify or name the sensations, simply fix your mind on observing them.

Take care never to generate a feeling of disappointment when the mind reacts or wanders, just accept the reality that the mind has reacted or wandered and gently bring it back to the breath.

If we do find that a major storm has arisen within us and we are beset with afflictive emotions such as addictive craving, anger, sadness or despair etc., returning the mind to the breath will have a very calming effect. Not only will it reduce the duration and intensity of our reactions, it will interrupt our damaging self-talk. It will remind us that we are living one moment at a time and that everything is in a constant state of change, including our difficult feelings and emotions.

With practice this simple meditation can help us develop the habit of observing ourselves, but more importantly it will help us become less reactive. The simple act of applying our mind to a chosen point of focus (the breath) allows us to step away from the mental storms of negative thinking and blind reaction.

If you would like to receive a FREE guided meditation mp3 to help you with this exercise please visit: www.thinkhappy.info/freegift.html

Step 3.

Gratitude

"Some people grumble that roses have thorns; I am grateful that thorns have roses." ~Alphonse Karr

Reframing your reality.

The other day I was having a cup of tea with a friend. She has had a pretty tough and challenging year and has a lot to process. She recently moved house for the first time in over a decade; she broke up a long-term relationship and has had a very ugly family situation crop up that she has to deal with.

While she looks to me to be doing pretty well she did confess that she was struggling a bit.

Recently she has been sticking her toe back in the romantic water and going on a few online dates. We were discussing the pros and cons of various internet dating sites, and whether the more casual swipe and pick or the more detailed profile driven model was more likely to result in a lasting relationship.

She had dated a few guys from the swipe and pick sites and it always seemed to get stuck in casual mode, so she had recently decided to give the more profile driven aps a try. With a heavy sigh she reported that she didn't like the profile model because she was being contacted by all these guys that she didn't think would be suitable for her; "my phone never stops beeping" she lamented.

I was a bit taken aback. She was upset because too many guys thought she was desirable and wanted to meet her? Digging a little deeper I asked her, why on earth would she look at it that way?

As it turned out the problem was she felt obliged to respond to every guy and the sheer magnitude of the task was weighing her down (whereas on the more casual swipe and pick model if you don't both pick each other there is no contact).

I pointed out that just as she was not duty bound do date every man who asked her out, nor was she duty bound to respond to someone just because they had contacted her *(sorry guys, I know it's harsh but a woman only has so many hours in a day)*.

I told her how lucky she was to be so attractive as to have such a wealth of choices and that every beep on her phone was just more evidence of how attractive and desirable she was. Her heavy weighted sigh disappeared and a huge smile appeared on her face.

Nothing had changed in her circumstances, but she had successfully reframed her reality from something that was dragging her down to something that was lifting her up. She had simply moved into a space of gratitude.

No matter what our circumstances, there is much in every life to be grateful for. Whether we choose to recognise it or not our lives have been filled with the efforts and goodwill of others.

If you are reading this book it is not only because someone took the time to teach you to read *(a gift that has opened up a world of knowledge and ideas for you)*, it is also due to the work of countless people throughout the ages; from Guttenberg *(who invented the first printing press)* to the electrical engineers, software designers, computer programmers, graphic artists, internet providers, printers and telecommunications companies that have made this book a reality today.

If we are not currently starving it is because of the efforts of all the farmers, refrigeration engineers, packaging manufacturers, storemen, truck drivers and shopkeepers that went into getting our food to us. If we are not currently naked it is because of the hard work of the cotton farmers, industrial chemists, designers, textile manufacturers, cutters, sewers, button and zip makers, shippers, shop assistants and countless others that are responsible for our having clothes.

There is no such thing a self made man. All of our abilities, comforts and successes are built upon the efforts of others. While some of us clearly have more than others, there is not one among us who has not benefited by the hand of another.

If we feel no gratitude to all those that have worked hard to provide us with the necessities of life we are robbing ourselves of the opportunity to feel the joy of our human connectedness. Gratitude is our heart's loving reminder that no matter where we go and what we do we carry a bounty of the world's largess with us.

In failing to recognise our gifts we are not only denying our own happiness, but the happiness of those to whom we would direct our gratitude. Fostering an attitude of gratitude is probably the single greatest thing we can do to immediately raise our ambient happiness level.

In a study conducted by Robert A. Emmons, Ph.D., at the University of California at Davis and Mike McCullough at the University of Miami, participants were randomly assigned one of three tasks. Each week, participants were asked to keep a short journal. One group were asked to briefly describe five things that had occurred that they were grateful for, another were asked to record five daily hassles, and the neutral group were asked to list five events that affected them, but were not instructed as to whether to focus on the positive or on the negative.

Ten weeks later the participants in the gratitude group felt considerably better about their lives and were 25% happier than those that had recorded their hassles. The gratitude group reported fewer health complaints, and even exercised an average of 1.5 hours more.

In a later study participants were asked to write a daily gratitude list. Not surprisingly, this led to a greater increase in gratitude than the weekly practice, but there was another significant benefit: the daily group reported offering more help or emotional support to other people, indicating that the gratitude exercise had increased their willingness to behave with kindness and care towards others.

Philip Watkins, a clinical psychologist at Eastern Washington University, found that clinically depressed individuals showed significantly lower levels (almost 50% less) of gratitude and appreciation than non-depressed controls. In fact several studies have shown an inverse correlation between depression and gratitude, suggesting that the more grateful we are the less likely we are to be depressed.

There is an old saying "if you have forgotten the language of gratitude, you'll never be on speaking terms with happiness".

Sometimes we mistakenly let the disappointment of unmet goals draw our focus away from the gifts we do have or we compare ourselves unfavourably to those that appear to have more. We spend all our time staring at the hole rather than the doughnut and in so doing we fail to recognise all that we do have.

There is no grace or happiness to be found in lamenting all the things in our lives that are not to our liking or dwelling on all the things we don't have. If we find there is something lacking in our life there is nothing wrong with pursuing it, but agonising over its absence or the outcome of our efforts will only make us miserable. It will not assist us in obtaining our goals.

Gratitude Exercises:

These gratitude exercises are possibly the simplest exercises you can do to increase your happiness. I recommend doing them daily.

Gratitude lists

Get a notebook and each day write down 5 things you are grateful for. They do not have to be huge things. It could be someone's friendship, it could be a good meal, it could be a warm scarf, it could even be that you can walk *(have recently broken my leg walking is now on my list)*; it could be anything.

In addition, as you go through your day take the time to let your mind wander over all the wonderful things people have done for you in your life.

Expressing gratitude

Tests have shown that expressing gratitude to someone who has impacted your life in a positive way can increase your happiness level by up to 20%.

This is a very easy thing to do, just pick up the phone or go and visit someone who has helped you or shown you kindness and thank them. Tell them how they have made your life better, and tell them how much you appreciate all their efforts. This amazingly simple exercise really works. Try it!

Step 4.

Forgiveness

"To err is human; to forgive, divine." - *Alexander Pope*

"The only way out of the labyrinth of suffering is to forgive."-- *John Green*

Forgiveness can be tricky. Sometimes the actions of others have such a profoundly painful impact on our lives that forgiving them can seem unthinkable.

Many times when people do things that upset, hurt or offend us we fail to realise that their bad behaviour is just a symptom of their unhappiness. Instead we take it personally and believe that their questionable behaviour is somehow about us, but this is never really the case.

People do what they do, and if you stand next to them they will do it to you!

It is quite common for us to believe that someone has set out to hurt us personally. You hear it all the time, *"why would she do that to me?"* or *"how could he be so cruel to me?"*

But a chronic philanderer is not cheating on you; he will cheat no matter who his current partner is. A thief is not stealing from you; she just wants the feelings she gets when acting out her acquisitive desires. A liar will lie no matter whom they are speaking to. A violent person will lash out at those close by, not because of who they are but simply because they are close at hand.

Like so many men of his generation my father went to fight in a war, an experience from which he never really recovered. On his return he became addicted to alcohol, and as a result did many questionable things. In the first 10 years after the war he married and started a family, but due to his inability to function properly he ran up so much debt that he simply couldn't see a way out. Ashamed and unable to face what he had done he forged his first wife's signature and borrowed all the equity out from under their jointly owned house. He then abandoned her with four children under the age of six.

When he met my mother a couple of years later he told her that his first wife had died of brain tumour and that he had no children. He then married my mother bigamously and proceeded to start his second family.

Forgiveness

When it looked like the law was catching up with him over his debts and his bigamy he decided that we needed to migrate, and so he moved our family to the other side of the world. Still terrified he was going to be caught he just couldn't settle down, so he did the same thing again. He forged my mother's signature and borrowed all the equity out from under the house they were building and took off.

My mother lost her entire life's savings and as a result she had a total nervous collapse. There she was, 40 years old living in a migrant hostel in a strange country, with no money, no family, no support and a two-year-old toddler and a six month old baby.

Even though she readily describes this period as the worst time in her life, she will happily admit it was the making of her.

After two weeks in the depths of despair she picked herself up and scraped herself back together. It was with the strongest of determination that she decided she would not only support herself *(not something that was expected of women or overly common in those days)*, but that she would never again let her self be crushed by the actions of another.

When she was contacted a year later by the police, who had found my father in a park, homeless, drunk and broke, she was faced with a tough decision. She could either abandon him to his fate *(which wasn't looking all that rosy)* or she could forgive him and try to help him get back onto his feet.

While my father never did really recover, my mother loved and cared for him for the next 24 years until he died. She never again owned anything jointly with him or let him get control of her money, but she forgave him. She understood that he was tragically broken and in all his terrible transgressions he was just trying to navigate a course through the deep anguish of his shattered life.

Admittedly there have been many questions raised as to whether or not she made the right choice, particularly given my father's questionable treatment of my sister and myself; but the reality is she does not regret her decision and even though it was tough for my sister and I, I do not regret her choice either.

The difficulties I experienced in my childhood are what have given me strength, focus and determination. Fine qualities I may not have felt so compelled to develop if not for the forgiving heart of my mother.

And as for my mother, she has spoken to us often of how broken my father was. How it was both his inability to forgive himself and the lack of available treatment for his war time PTSD that had led him to drink, rage and lash out at those around him. She would often point to his kindness towards animals as a glimpse into his true nature.

We all have relationships with people who behave badly at some point, and even if we cannot continue to have them present in our lives it is important to recognise the root cause of their questionable behaviours.

The fact is all negative behaviours stem from a deep misery in the perpetrator, yet we react as if they were specifically designed to hurt us.

When someone behaves badly it is crucially important to recognise that they are not actually "doing it to us" personally and that anyone behaving in an antisocial manner is suffering equally, if not more than their victims.

When someone behaves poorly it is always because they have been knocked off their ethical behavioural centre by an overwhelming rush of afflictive emotions, such as anxiety, greed, lust, anger, ill will or animosity and are suffering an overload of craving or aversion from which they are fighting to escape.

When someone is reacting and consequently behaving badly it is never really about us. We can never control or regulate the behaviour of others, particularly when their rationality has been swept away by an emotional storm. We can request, we can suggest, we can set an example, we can attempt to influence and persuade, but ultimately it is beyond our control.

Once one truly understands that people only behave badly when they themselves are suffering, adding to their misery with our own, or flaying them with our anger hardly seems like an appropriate or helpful response. It will not improve their condition or behaviour and it will undoubtedly have a negative impact on ours.

This is not to say that one should blithely accept the abuses of others, far from it. If one is able *(and it is safe to do so)*, one should always try to stop an abuser from harming themselves or others. If it is not safe to intervene one should seek to secure the safety of those present as best one can and notify the appropriate authorities.

While others may need protection from someone who has lost the balance of their mind and is acting out, the perpetrator also needs help and protection.

There is no practical purpose to be served by replaying their transgressions over and over on the stage of our minds, repeatedly drawing ourselves back into the emotional maelstrom and filling our minds with judgement and anger.

If someone has acted inappropriately and harmed others it is far more helpful to recognise that their actions are born out of their suffering and proceed to do all we can to help restore them to a stable and harmonious state.

To push more suffering upon them will only exacerbate their problems and perpetuate their harmful behaviour. Just as we would not want to be judged by our lowest moments, so we should refrain from closing our hearts to others who have also crossed over a line at some point.

That does not mean we have to open the door to abusive people or invite poor behaviour into our lives; it simply means that we should not harbour any anger, ill will or resentment towards people who, *(in reacting to their own misery)*, have caused damage to others.

If someone is habitually losing the balance of their mind and represents a threat to those around them, we may need to remove them from our lives, or they may need to be incarcerated. In such cases we should know that it is the greatest act of care to prevent someone from causing harm; but in so doing we should wish not them any ill. We should instead wish them inner peace and happiness, for their good as well as the good of others.

Self Forgiveness

If we are honest with ourselves we have to know that it is not just others who are prone to episodes of bad behaviour. We all get overwhelmed by afflictive emotions sometimes and behave in ways that we later come to regret. Admittedly some people manage their emotional storms better than others, but everyone transgresses from time to time.

But when we react badly and breach our moral boundaries it can lead to a deeply ruptured sense of self, resulting in crippling levels of guilt, self-recrimination, addiction, violent outbursts, criminality, depression and even suicide.

Occasionally people transgress their own moral boundaries because circumstance has compelled them to do so. This is frequently the case with returning soldiers; war often requires people to do things that they find morally reprehensible and are subsequently unable to reconcile.

If we do not forgive ourselves our transgressions have the capacity to infect the core of our being to the point where happiness is simply impossible. Our only hope for liberation is in accepting the reality of our actions, forgiving ourselves and taking a strong determination to gain a greater mastery over our mind so that we can do better in future.

The story of my father is a case in point. Had he been able to forgive himself the transgressions of his war years he would have most likely been able to live a peaceful happy life, but the guilt and self-recrimination that he carried lead to progressively worse and worse behaviours; and resulted in a lot of damage to himself, his families and loved ones.

Seeking the pardon of others

None of us are perfect people. We all make mistakes and do things that hurt and harm others. If we truly allow ourselves to take that fact on board it can lead to overwhelming feelings of guilt and shame, which not only stands in the way of our happiness but may cause us to act poorly again in the future.

If we recognise that we have acted badly we need to own it wholly and not try and blame others for our behaviours. We also need to find a way to resolve the situation so it doesn't carry forward and affect our future thinking and behaviour.

The first step on that road is to acknowledge that we have behaved badly and to apologise. It takes much greater strength of character to acknowledge we have done something wrong and apologise than to avoid taking any responsibility.

Not being able to apologise is a sign that someone is unable to face the reality of his own imperfection, however we all need to face that reality if we are ever to be truly happy.

Forgiveness

When we ask others for their forgiveness we have to accept that we may not get it. Whether they are able to forgive us or not is an issue for them, it is not something we can force or control. If they find they are unable to forgive us, we should take that as a sign that they are in still in great pain and try to have as much compassion and goodwill for them as we can.

Apologising for our poor behaviour is something we must learn to do in order to become mature adults, but that does not mean we can force others to accept our apology.

No-one owes us a continued place in their life. We cannot and should not ever try to force our presence in someone else's life. No matter how painful we may find it, if our behaviour has caused someone to end their association with us we need to respect their choice and accept it gracefully.

At times we all find it difficult to practice forgiveness, but if we do not do it we only end up poisoning our hearts. In forgiving we are not only freeing ourselves from our anger, ill will, hatred and animosity, we are preventing our own misery from overpowering us and causing us to behave badly in future. In forgiving we are breaking the cycle our own misery.

The weak can never forgive. Forgiveness is the attribute of the strong – Mahatma Ghandi

Forgiveness is not something you can give to others; it is something you hold in your heart for all the suffering caused by yourself and others. It is the profound knowing that it is only the misery of craving, aversion and ignorance that causes people to act against the wellbeing of themselves or others.

Forgiveness is the act of pardoning ourselves for any suffering we may have caused others and the deeply held wish that all those who have harmed us be relieved of their suffering. This wish is not just for their own good; it is for the good of anyone who may come in contact with them in future.

Exercise: Practicing forgiveness.

When the wrongdoings of others come to mind try to imagine the suffering that lead to their transgressions. Try to remember that they were suffering and reacting in ignorance and as much as they may have hurt us, they were also making themselves miserable with their reactions. With this in mind pardon them and wish them well.

For self-forgiveness simply direct the process towards your self. Understand that at the time of your transgression you were suffering and had lost the balance of your mind. Commit yourself again to increasing your mastery of your mind, so you may in future choose a different course when afflictive emotions arise.

In situations, such as war, where the choice to act in a noble fashion was not available to you, know that you where under extreme duress and highly reactive and thus you did the best you could in the circumstances. With this in mind pardon yourself and continue to practice to strengthen your mind.

Step 5.

Generosity

"You catch nothing with a closed fist" - *Anonymous.*

"No one has ever become poor by giving." - *Anne Frank*

We live in an age of self-obsession. We are so concerned with ourselves, our image, our desires or what others think of us that we often fail to consider the situation of others. We are so busy propping ourselves up and catering to our own comforts and desires that we don't notice the real, tangible needs of others.

We view those that have very little with suspicion, worried that they might try to carve off a bit of what is ours for themselves. We jealously guard our wealth and time, as if giving some of it away would leave us without enough to meet our needs.

This reluctance to give of ourselves is so ingrained in our society that the fact that charity does a lot more for the giver than it can ever do for the receiver has become something of a well kept secret.

But when we direct our focus solely to the meeting of our own desires we become trapped in an endless spiral of craving. We never reach a point of satisfaction because every goal we achieve loses its taste the moment it is won. Our lives become a festival of ever-receding goal posts. We become miserable and agitated because no matter how much we get it is never enough to satisfy our craving. Time and time again we convince ourselves that the next victory, the next acquisition, the next conquest will be the one that will deliver us true and lasting happiness, but it never is.

In helping others there is connectedness, purpose and love. Generosity is the living embodiment of faith. We have all that we need and some to spare. There is great power and great joy in serving others.

There are literally thousands of stories out there of people who give of themselves, either financially or with their time to make life better for others. Every time one such story makes onto the news there is always beaming smiles on the faces of both the givers and the recipients.

Here are a couple of stories of people who have actively practised generosity to inspire you.

The Dumpster Diver

On thanksgiving a homeless man, Joel Hartman was digging in the dumpster outside of the Omni Hotel in Atlanta when he found a wallet. He took the wallet to the hotel reception to give back to the guest. The hotel manager was so struck by Hartman's honesty that he gave him a room for the weekend, free room service, a new wardrobe and a make-over.

But that's not the end of the story. When the media got hold of the story, his family, who had been looking for him for years, finally found him. As a result Hartman will now be getting medical treatment that he needs for his ADHD.

The Big Tipper

When Aaron Collins died, his will stated that his family should go out to dinner and leave an "awesome tip".

The first time his brother left a huge gratuity the story went viral and donations started to pour in for the family to go out and leave more tips in the memory of their Beloved Aaron.

They have received about $50,000. since then, and his brother has been travelling around the country leaving a huge tip in each state.

His brother Seth said "It's rewarding because I get to make their day and hopefully inspire generosity in that person," "Beyond that, creating this legacy for my brother and creating these pockets of people all around the world who know about him and will always remember him."

Exercise: Practicing Generosity

Practicing generosity doesn't just mean giving to others in a material sense. Clearly not everyone has the resources to give money or goods but everyone has the capacity to act generously towards others.

There are many ways to give selfless service. Help with a problem, the gift of time or effort, a sympathetic ear or a kind word. We all have to capacity to help others in some way. Even picking up a piece of rubbish off the street and placing it in the bin is an act of generosity, as it is giving of one's time and energy to make things better for us all.

Practising generosity is simply carrying the mindset of "how can I help?" and acting on the opportunities that present themselves.

Being mindful and on the lookout for ways to make a positive difference will make you a far happier person than obsessing over what you can carve off for yourself. This is what the social worker who offered the week's work in the homeless kitchen as a first prize and the luxury car as the second prize understood; we are at our happiest when we are able to act with generosity towards others.

There are so many things you can do to give generously. There is the movement for paying for lunch or a coffee for a homeless person at your local cafe. For example Rosa's Fresh Pizza, a Philadelphia pizza shop has given away more than 8,400 slices of pizza to the needy in just over a year in a pay-it-forward campaign.

You could visit a lonely elderly person in hospital or clean up the trash in your neighbourhood park.

You could offer to assist at the local school or set up a charity pledge. You could donate quality clothes and blankets to outreach programs or you could lend your skills, whatever they may be, to someone in need.

Anything you can think of that will help others will also help make you a happier person.

Step 6.

Kindness and Compassion

Compassion

If you want others to be happy, practice compassion. If you want to be happy, practice compassion. - Dalai Lama

Compassion is a feeling of deep sympathy for another who is stricken by misfortune, accompanied by a strong desire to alleviate their suffering.

The first step in cultivating compassion is to develop empathy for your fellow human beings, as empathy is the gatekeeper of compassion. Empathy is the act of applying our imagination to the suffering of others. Imagining what it must be like to walk in their shoes, to suffer as they suffer.

Exercise: Practising compassion

When you know of something terrible that has happened to a loved one, try to imagine the pain they are going through. Imagine their suffering in as much detail as possible. Continue to extend this practice outward, imagining the suffering of others you know and then out toward the suffering of strangers and then out further to all living things.

Once you can truly empathize with others, understanding their humanity and suffering, the next step is to wish for them to be free from suffering.

Open your heart to them and cultivate the feeling that you want their suffering to end; reflect on that feeling. That is the feeling that you want to develop and with practice that feeling can be nurtured and grow.

Kindness

"Be kind, for everyone you meet is fighting a harder battle." - Plato

"Three things in human life are important: the first is to be kind; the second is to be kind; and the third is to be kind." - Henry James

During a recent flood disaster, the news did a spot interviewing people in the process of filling sand bags for their neighbours. You could see these people felt purposeful, empowered and deeply happy. Not because they could control the flood, but because they were fully focused on what they COULD achieve for the good of their neighbours!

If your mind is constantly focused on "all the trouble in your world", you cannot feel your natural power. When your mind is so full of what's wrong there is simply no room for truly understanding and appreciating what you can achieve. Everyone has the power to do something to make life a little better for somebody else.

Doing for others is expansive and exhilarating, and it makes us happy!

Exercise: Practicing kindness

The practice of kindness is not difficult. It can be as easy as offering a smile or a kind word, doing an errand or chore, or just talking through a problem with another person.

At the risk of repeating myself we all have the power to make the world a little better for someone else. In doing some small kindness each day to help ease the suffering of others we are exercising one of the greatest powers we have.

It is not even necessary that someone knows that you have acted for their benefit. Sometimes a random act of kindness is the greatest gift you can give. A random anonymous act of kindness tells the recipient that the world is not a cold and uncaring place. It reminds the recipient that there are people out there who will render assistance without expecting anything in return. A random act of kindness can actually restore someone's faith in the world... now that's a super power!

Once you have become good at this, find a way to make it a daily practice, and eventually even a several times a day practice. You will be amazed by the power you have to effect peoples lives for the better.

If you are struggling to think of some act of kindness you might try visiting ask.io, www.Ask.io is a website created to get people to engage in small acts of kindness. Each week the site posts a different "favour" from sending birthday cards to sick person to donating money to "Dogs in Harmony" an organization which cares for ailing canines.

"My goal with this website is simply to do small things for those who are in need of a personal favour," writes creator Mike Carson.

Step 7:

Active Self Care

If we truly want to be happy it is not enough to work solely on managing our minds; we must also maintain our physical health and our relationships as well.

If our relationships are tense and full of conflict, or if our bodies are weak, ill or overburdened with stimulants, it is far more difficult for us to be calm and happy. Many of the strategies and crutches we use to build a damn against our more difficult feelings are highly toxic to our bodies and our minds and need to be addressed if we are to achieve lasting changes in our lives.

Improving our diet and exercise regime provides an excellent foundation for making sustained changes in our thinking, and subsequently in our happiness levels.

While we should try to reduce any overconsumption of junk food, drugs, alcohol and cigarettes and reduce any acting out of compulsive behaviours, it is not helpful to stress ourselves out with an over restrictive list of dos and don'ts.

For example if your diet is questionable it may be too much to try and fix it all at once. Rather if we choose one small aspect of our diet - such as our soda consumption - and start by eliminating or reducing our intake until we are accustomed to our new level. Once we have integrated that change and it has become largely effortless we can move on to the next modification. Like this, patiently and persistently we can turn our bad habits around.

For example, making small incremental improvements like getting off the bus one stop early or parking at the back of the lot when we do the shopping so we have to walk a bit further might be a relaxed way to start incorporating more exercise into our lives.

Try replacing half your daily tea or coffee with water or substituting a chocolate bar with a piece of fruit. Not only will it improve your health, it will save you money and reduce your environmental footprint.

Admittedly there are some things we may need to go cold turkey on, such as anything that leads us into compulsive behaviours or addictive spirals, but we don't need to tackle all our bad habits at once; it is far better for us to move gently towards progressively higher and higher levels of self care.

Physical Exercise:

While the physical benefits of exercise are well known, including everything from weight loss, metabolic stimulation, increased muscle definition, improved circulation, improved bone density to increased strength and endurance, exercise can also have a profound impact on your happiness levels. I know from my own experience that nothing shakes off my bad mood better than going for a swim.

Exercise stimulates the brain and releases endorphins, (chemicals known to produce the feelings of euphoria that are sometimes referred to as the "runner's high.") and endorphins subsequently trigger the release of hormones, such as norepinephrine, which are known to enhance mood and create an elevated sense of wellbeing.

Exercise is fantastic for relieving and reducing stress. When we exercise, our bodies burn the stress hormone cortisol. High cortisol levels cause nervousness, anxiety, decreased motivation and immune function so any cortisol you can burn off is only going to leave you feeling lighter. As little as 30 minutes of moderate-intensity exercise, like gentle walking, can help reduce depression and anger.

Depending on your fitness level you may need to consult a doctor before beginning a regular formal exercise regime, but even a modest daily walk is a great place to begin. Start with five to ten minuets and build up from there.

Improving your diet:

Diet has a profound effect on our mood. As the old saying goes "you are what you eat", so if we eat a lot of junk and fast foods we cannot expect that we are going to feel great.

Apart from the obvious misery of dietary and lifestyle induced diseases such as certain cancers, diabetes, gout, osteoarthritis, allergies etc., a poor diet can lead to addictive compulsive behaviours and motivational and mood disorders.

Active Self Care

While this is clearly not a diet book, I can totally recommend that you make your best efforts to choose foods that promote good health. This means reducing your intake of processed foods, trans fats and sugars etc., and increasing the amount of fresh fruit and vegetables you consume.

If you can make the conscious effort to eat well for about three weeks you should notice a general improvement in your mood. Also after three weeks the dietary improvements you have made will start to become a habitual way of eating that you won't want to give up.

Finding community:

Human beings are social beings. To survive and thrive we need to be part of a broader social group.

There are many places we can find social connectedness. Depending on our needs and interests we may find a religious or spiritual assembly, a 12 step program, a volunteer organisation, a support group or a special interest group that can serve our needs for inclusion and community.

The website www.meetup.com has local group listings for almost every imaginable interest, so if you are having trouble finding your tribe it could be a great place to start.

If you are wrestling with anxiety, depression, PTSD, addiction or abuse I highly recommend committing to some kind of group, as the support and love of a community is an invaluable resource while working towards healing and recovery.

Pain Management:

For some people their unhappiness is either caused or compounded by the fact they suffer acute or chronic pain. Pain-killers can only do so much and many of them have damaging side effects.

Acute pain comes on suddenly, it can pass quickly or last for weeks or even months but will go away once the root cause has been addressed.

Chronic pain may result from an injury or infection or it may even be psychogenic, (meaning that it is not related to injury). Chronic pain is a pain that persists for months or years and often has a profound affect on your physical and emotional wellbeing.

Identifying which type of pain you have and seeking the appropriate medical treatment is the first step in taking control of the situation. Beyond that there are a number of things that you can do that can assist you in dealing with chronic or overpowering pain.

Staying Hydrated:

According to the Mayo Clinic dehydration may aggravate some chronic conditions like headaches and back pain.

The diuretic effect of coffee, soda or juice makes them poor a choice for increased hydration, whereas water keeps you hydrated without the extra calories, sodium or caffeine.

Eating Well

An easy-to-digest diet free from processed foods can alleviate inflammation. Sugar is known to be inflammatory and as such should be kept to a minimum but low-sugar fruits like cherries, strawberries, blueberries, cranberries, plums and pineapple are good choices. Try to stay away from fruit juices as they have a high sugar load but no fibre.

You may also want to cut down on high-fat red meat, wheat products, processed foods, red wine, chocolate, coffee, tea and soda.

The Indian yellow spice "turmeric" is amazing! Turmeric contains curcumin, which naturally reduces inflammation in the body without harming the liver or kidneys. One teaspoon mixed in half a glass of water daily has been shown to be as effective as some steroids in reducing pain and inflammatory conditions. (I take this myself for my hay fever, and my mother takes it for her arthritis; and it really works).

Leafy greens and foods that are high in omega-3 fatty acids may also help alleviate inflammation.

A mental exercise for dealing with pain.

The feelings and sensations we experience as pain can have a vicelike grip on our attention, making it extremely difficult for us to do anything else other than be aware that we are in pain. As acute pain can totally dominate our mind's focus it is important that we try to develop and maintain the right kind of awareness when painful sensations arise.

I know by my own experience that when one reacts with hatred and aversion to painful sensation the pain one experiences is greatly increased. Conversely when you are able to observe painful sensations without reacting to them, the sensations may continue and stay for some time but one is no longer distressed or agitated by them.

Observing painful sensations without reaction or resistance is not easy but it is possible. Admittedly it takes practice, but if one is beset with chronic pain it is a skillset well worth developing.

When painful sensations are overwhelming try to sit quietly and comfortably and focus on your breath using the technique outlined in step 2.

After a minute or two turn your attention to the site of your pain. Making every effort not to react take your mind into the centre of the pain and see what physical sensations are present. Try to analyse the sensations dispassionately, like a doctor examining someone else's pain. Try to identify the centre of the pain, noting whether the pain is dull or sharp, throbbing or itching, just observe its nature, without reaction.

Often times you will find that as you bring your mind into the centre of the pain, the sensations will either seem to run away from you (so you have to chase them around with your mind's eye) or they will dissolve and dissipate.

After a moment or two move your attention out from the centre of the pain and examine the surrounding area. Try to identify where the pain starts and where it stops. Try to feel the different types and gradations of sensation as you move you attention throughout the area.

This is a deceptively simple exercise that is quite difficult to master, so it is perfectly natural to expect that we will still get overwhelmed by our painful sensation from time to time. If you find that your mind is very reactive and you are unable to observe the sensations objectively, simply return your attention to the breath and wait for the storm to pass, then quietly try again.

If you practice this exercise regularly you will find that your mind will automatically become less reactive and that you will be able to function better mentally in spite of your pain.

Another other somewhat surprising thing you may find is that the painful sensations by themselves are not all that distressing. It is only when the mind reacts with hatred towards those sensations that the painful sensations become unbearable. If we sit quietly, without reaction and simply watch them flow by they do not overpower us. However if we dive into the river and try to control the flow we will be swept away into a sea of distress.

This exercise is also very helpful with children that have had a fall and are in distress. Simply sit the child down and ask them to describe their pain to you in intricate detail. Ask them where the centre of their pain is. Ask them where it starts and stops, is it sharp or dull, tingling itching? I have witnessed this exercise having a profoundly calming effect on distressed children.

Like choosing to focus on your breath, choosing to focus on your bodily sensations is an act of directing your mind according to your wishes rather that allowing your mind to just flail about in uncontrolled reaction. The practice of wilful observation and analysis is so powerful because it moves the mind out of blind reaction and into objective, rational observation.

Mental Illness

While it is quite common for people affected by mental illness to feel isolated and alone, mental illness is actually staggeringly common. To give you some sense of how common it is the National Alliance on Mental Illness provides the following statistics for the USA.

One in four adults (approximately 61.5 million Americans) experiences mental illness in a given year.

One in 17 -about 13.6 million- live with a serious mental illness such as schizophrenia, major depression or bipolar disorder.

Approximately 20% of youth ages 13 to 18 experience severe mental disorders in a given year. For ages 8 to 15, the estimate is 13%.

Approximately 1.1% of American adults -about 2.4 million people- live with schizophrenia.

Approximately 2.6% of American adults 6.1 million people live with bipolar disorder. 4,5

Approximately 6.7%of American adults -about 14.8 million people- live with major depression.

Approximately 18.1% of American adults -about 42 million people- live with anxiety disorders such as panic disorder, obsessive-compulsive disorder (OCD), posttraumatic stress disorder (PTSD), generalized anxiety disorder and phobias.

About 9.2 million adults have co-occurring mental health and addiction disorders.

Approximately 26% of homeless adults staying in shelters live with serious mental illness and an estimated 46% live with severe mental illness and/or substance use disorders.

Approximately 20% of state prisoners and 21% of local jail prisoners have "a recent history" of a mental health condition.

70% of youth in juvenile justice systems have at least one mental health condition and at least 20% live with a severe mental illness.

Given these statistics it is safe to say that if you are in a room with three other people you could expect that at least one of you will have suffered a bout of mental illness within the last 12 months.

Mental illness is often overly stigmatised and poorly understood. While some serious mental illnesses can affect a person's mood and behaviour if left untreated they do not alter the nature or character of a person. A loving kind person with a mental illness is still a loving and kind person and as such we should always make the effort to see the real person, not just the symptoms of their disease.

In many cases serious mental illness has a biological underpinning that can be treated with medication, however many milder mental disorders such as low-level depression and anxiety can be simply be the product of the changes in body chemistry that occur as a result of toxic thinking.

Regardless of the nature or severity of one's mental illness practicing good mental habits will inevitably lead to increased levels of happiness. Any technique that teaches us how to manage our minds, think in more helpful and constructive ways and be less reactive can only be beneficial.

The practices outlined in this book are not replacements for any medical treatments, but rather should be viewed as an adjunct to any medication, or professional treatment regime.

Resources

I have included this section as a guide to those who may be seeking additional help and resources in their quest for a happier, more self-determined life. I highly recommend that you take full advantage of everything that is available to help you on your journey

Cognitive Behavioural Therapy

Cognitive behavioural therapy is the formal name given by physiologists in the UK to the therapeutic exercises and treatments that are based around changing ones patterns of thinking.

While this treatment model is widely available on a paid one to one basis, there are many wonderful free resources and workbooks available on line.

http://www.getselfhelp.co.uk/

http://www.feelingbetternow.com/uk/disorder_cbt.asp

http://serene.me.uk/

Addiction and Recovery Programs

The American Society of Addiction Medicine and the National Institute on Drug Abuse have endorsed rational and secular approaches such as Smart Recovery as constituting "evidence based practice". However some mental health professionals, addiction councillors and therapists believe rational means, while useful, do not work by themselves for addicts and alcoholics because they do not fully address all the facets of the illness of addiction.

Personally I think it is a matter for each individual to decide for herself.

Rational and Secular Programs

Religious or spiritual based programs are unlikely to gain traction with committed rationalists. The following is a list of addiction programs that provide a range of fully inclusive options for the spiritually unaffiliated.

I have no personal knowledge of the detail or efficacy of these programs and would recommend any one who is interested in these should make their own enquiries.

Addiction Alternatives

(www.addictionalternatives.com)

Science based solutions, not 12-step based methods, are used to help manage addictive behaviours for life. The site includes online self-assessment tests, useful information on the philosophy of behaviour change, an extensive list of alternative treatment approaches to addiction and a variety of addiction treatment professional services including Reduction Training and Abstinence Training.

Exposure Response Prevention

(www.killthecraving.com)

ERP® is a behavioural therapy technique that systematically exposes an addict to simulated versions of their drugs of choice and the equipment related to its use in order to elicit powerful cravings.

As the addict learns to observe their cravings and triggers without giving into them, the desire to use becomes progressively weaker until it no longer holds any power over the addict. ERP® therapy leads to increased self-control and confidence, which results in a reduced likelihood of relapse.

ERP® can be done through photo cards (using their book "Kill The Craving" and their website) or with a trained therapist (call 1-888-8-CARE-4U for more information about this version of ERP®).

An outcome study documenting the effectiveness of ERP® is available on their website.

LifeRing Secular Recovery

(www.unhooked.com)

This non-religious recovery network is based on a group process self-help system of recovery. The website provides a national meeting list organised by state, news bulletins, online scientific articles, a chat room with daily online meetings, reviews of recovery books and extensive links organised by topic such as recovery groups, government/academic sites and various approaches to healing.

Rational Recovery

www.rational.org

Rational Recovery embraces the idea of immediate self-recovery from addiction through the learned skill of planned abstinence. Abstinence is facilitated by using an easily-learned method called Addictive Voice Recognition Technique® (AVRT). There is no religious or spiritual component to this method of recovery. The web site offers an online course on AVRT, an online bookstore offering Rational Recovery books, audiotapes, videotapes, discussion forums, articles and essays.

Secular Organizations for Sobriety (SOS)

www.secularsobriety.org

SOS provides a non-religious path to sobriety through a network of local group meetings. Their web site offers a 24 hour online real-time chat meeting using voice or type, a meeting locator for groups in the U.S. and Europe, a sobriety tool kit, recommended readings and more.

SMART Recovery

www.smartrecovery.org

SMART Recovery is a nationwide not-for-profit organization that provides free self-help support groups to people who want to abstain from addictive behaviour. Participants learn tools for addiction recovery based on the latest scientific research and participate in a worldwide community that includes free, self-empowering, science-based mutual help groups.

SMART Recovery sponsors face-to-face meetings around the world, and daily online meetings. In addition, they offer an online message board and 24/7 chat rooms where you can get addiction recovery support.

The program is based on cognitive, behavioural and educational methods that seek to change the beliefs and attitudes that can lead to addictive behaviour. The site has online recovery meetings, a message board, Internet discussion groups, a meeting list and recommended reading.

The 4-Point Program helps people recover from all types of addiction and addictive behaviours, including: drug abuse, drug addiction, substance abuse, alcohol abuse, gambling addiction, cocaine addiction, prescription drug abuse, sexual addiction and problem addiction to other substances and activities.

Spiritual based Recovery Programs

The most well know spiritually based programs are the 12 step programs. As most people are aware of the basics of the 12 step system I am not going to go into it in detail here, but rather I have listed the links to their web sites, where more information can easily be obtained.

Alcoholics Anonymous

http://www.aa.org/

Narcotics Anonymous

https://www.na.org/

Overeaters Anonymous

http://www.oa.org.au/

Gamblers Anonymous

http://www.gamblersanonymous.org/ga/

Sex Addicts Anonymous

https://saa-recovery.org/

Nicotine Anonymous

https://nicotine-anonymous.org/

Mindfulness and Meditation Courses

Mindfulness meditation is an adaptation of vipassana meditation in which one learns to become mindful through practicing the intentional, non-judgmental focusing of one's attention on the emotions, thoughts and sensations occurring throughout the body in the present moment.

Through mindfulness the practitioner adopts a mental position that allows them to separate any given experience from an associated emotion, a practice that can enable practitioners to find a skilful or mindful response to any given situation.

UCLA Mindful Awareness Research Centre

http://marc.ucla.edu/body.cfm?id=22

This website provides a number of free guided mindfulness meditations. This is an excellent resource.

Mindful Schools

www.mindfulschools.org

Mindful Schools offer online training courses to adults with a focus on training teachers to bring mindfulness training into schools.

Vipassana Meditation

http://www.dhamma.org/en-US/index

If you are fortunate enough to have the time to take a free 10 day residential mediation course I highly recommend you do. There is nothing in my search for happiness that has had such a profound effect on my personal progress and quality of life as learning this meditation technique.

There are no charges for the courses - not even to cover the cost of food and accommodation. All expenses are met by donations from people who, having completed a course and experienced the benefits of Vipassana, wish to give others the opportunity to also benefit. Vipassana courses are available throughout the world with over 160 residential course centres and additional courses being offered at over 120 non-course centres.

Guidelines for practice

The exercises contained in this book are all simple, practical tools that you can use to achieve a greater level of happiness. Have confidence that if you practice these exercises with any consistency you will see wonderful results. Work patiently and persistently, for just as it takes time to train a wild horse so it takes time to train our minds.

There will still be days when you are highly reactive or taken by afflictive emotion and you need to be extra gentle with your self. Remember that none of us are perfect and we all get overpowered by emotional storms now and again. Smilingly forgive yourself and move on with a determination to try and do better next time.

There is absolutely no doubt that any positive practices or disciplines you adopt will eventually bear fruit. For some the harvest will come quickly, for others it may take a little longer. Be patient and have faith. No harm can ever come to you from actively practicing forgiveness, kindness, compassion, generosity, gratitude, mindfulness, and self-care.

Hope for PTSD sufferers.

Having grown up with a father suffering PSTD and having suffered from it myself I am acutely aware of how debilitating it can be. The range of therapies currently available have been somewhat random in their efficacy, offering substantial recovery to some sufferers while others remain much as they were before treatment.

While the research is still in its infancy there is now genuine cause for hope with a real and substantive cure for the condition looking possible.

Recently developments in the study of memory have shown that memory recall works quite differently to what was previously thought. The research suggests that when we actively recall a memory we move it out of long-term storage and into a temporary buffer where we are able to interact with it. Once we have finished "looking at" that memory we then put it back into long-term storage. Kind of like removing a file from a cabinet and spreading it out on our desk so we can look at it, packing up and filing it away again.

The thing is that when we put that memory back into the filing cabinet it never goes back in exactly the same way it came out. Slight changes are inevitably made while we interacting with it, resulting in our memories gradually distorting over time.

In PTSD sufferers, some memories have a very traumatic emotional component, which is also bought to the surface whenever the memory is recalled, which can retrigger the emotional component of the trauma all over again. (This is believed to be the reason counselling in aftermath of a traumatic event can actually be damaging to some people).

However new research is suggesting that by deliberately bringing traumatic memories to the fore in a safe and pleasant environment, it may be possible to alter the emotional component of those memories while they are in active recall and send them back to the long term memory without the traumatic emotional charge.

This would leave the sufferer with an intact memory of the event without the crippling emotional component.

More information on this stunning new research can be found in an article from the Smithsonian by following the link below.

http://bit.ly/1N5Wi2l

Author's Note

I would like to take just a moment to personally thank you for reading this book. Your time is so precious and I feel both honoured and privileged that you have deemed this work worthy of your time and attention.

It is my sincere hope that you may have found something within these pages that can help you in both your personal relationships and your day-to-day life.

If you have found value in this book it would be greatly appreciated if you could help others find it so that they too can benefit. Leaving a review on Amazon only takes a few moments but it is extremely helpful in guiding others (who may also benefit from it) towards this book. You can review this book on the following link and scrolling down to the review section.

https://www.amazon.com/dp/B00X52GKSQ

Be Happy

Margaret

www.ingramcontent.com/pod-product-compliance
Lightning Source LLC
LaVergne TN
LVHW011718060526
838200LV00051B/2946